THE NEW CIVIL WAR BOOK

by
Judy Cheney

Cover art by Sylvia Jones
Map & Line Drawings by Kathleen B. Pridgen
SPECIAL THANKS TO

Harper's Weekly
Bennett Place State Historic Site
...and the many Editors who
helped make this book possible.

©Copyright & Distribution by
Aerial Photography Services, Inc.
2300 Dunavant Street
Charlotte, North Carolina 28203

I.S.B.N. 0-936672-16-1
Library of Congress Catalog Card Number
83-071251

*This book is dedicated
to the thousands of Soldiers and many others
who gave their lives during the Civil War.*

TABLE OF CONTENTS

The Civil War .... 1 and 2
Brief Chronology of the War .... 3 thru 6
Dramatis Personae .... 7 thru 15
Women and the War .... 16 and 17
Negroes During the War .... 18 thru 20
Naval Highlights of the War .... 21 thru 24
Medical Care 25
Centerfold Map of the Battles
   of the Civil War .... 26 and 27
Civil War Prisons 28
Prose, Poetry and Songs of the Civil War .... 29 thru 45
Bennett Place Memorial .... 46 and 47
Quick Reference Guide .... 48 thru 54
Suggested Reading and Bio 55

THE CIVIL WAR

The War Between the United States - also called The War of Rebellion, The War of Secession, The War for Southern Independence, or the Civil War (April 12, 1861 - May 26, 1865) was the most tragic episode in the history of the American nation. It was a conflict in which brother fought against brother, father against son, friend against friend and spies operated against family and neighbors. The family and friendships ties were so strong that Confederate and Union sentries often met in "No Man's Land" during the lulls in the fighting to exchange tobacco, coffee and news of home...

What were the reasons that brother turned against brother and against the nation their fathers had founded? The Civil War had many causes. Men in the north differed with southerners on questions of tariff, territories, slavery, immigration, states rights and railroad routes. The north was industrial and commercial, urban and energetic, with Puritan zeal for humanitarian causes such as abolition and yankee zest for expansion and growth.

In the bustling world of the mid-nineteenth century, the southern dream of a realm of slave-holding states stretching across the lower half of the continent was an anomaly, doomed to failure. In reality the south was rural, undeveloped, underpopulated and resistant to change. The profits of the region's one-crop cotton economy depended on slave labor. The area had little industry, shipping, commerce or manpower to wage war against the northern states and all their resources.

In its scope the Civil War became one of the greatest struggles in history. More Americans lost their lives than in World War II. Over 10,000 battles, skirmishes, operations and engagements (not counting naval actions) were fought. There were spectacular battles, riotous raids and marches of devastation across vast areas of the southern landscape. Technological advances made it the first modern war, with extensive use of railroads, field telegraph, armored ships, mines and attempts at balloon surveillance and submarines. Engineer corps performed ingenious feats on both sides. The personal valour of the men who fought the war, north and south, was remarkable. Ordinary soldiers gave "The Last Full Measure" for something they valued more than life.

Twenty years after his service as a young captain under General Lew Wallace, Oliver Wendell Holmes, Jr., spoke of the men of his day, "The generation that carried on the war has been set aside by it's experience, through our great good fortune, in our youth our hearts were touched with fire. It was given to us to learn at the outset that life is a profound and passionate thing... we have seen with our own eyes, beyond and above the gold fields, the snowy heights of honor, and it is for us to bear the report to those who come after us...

The history of the United States of America as "One Nation Indivisible" began at Appomattox Courthouse. The two great generals, Ulysses S. Grant & Robert E. Lee, made the peace with honor; the victors and the vanquished accepted it with grace and reconciliation. Our greatest national tragedy ended with the beginning of our more perfect union. We who have "come after" owe that gallant generation our deepest gratitude.

****

BRIEF CHRONOLOGY OF THE CIVIL WAR

1859

October - John Brown's raid on Harper's Ferry.

1860

November - Abraham Lincoln elected President.

December - South Carolina secedes from the Union.

1861

January-February - Mississippi, Florida, Alabama, Georgia, Louisiana and Texas secede from the Union. Delegates from seven seceding states meet in Montgomery, Alabama to form the Confederate States of America and elect Jefferson Davis President.

April - After failure to find a peaceful settlement, the Confederates fire on Fort Sumter in Charleston Harbor. The Union surrenders the Fort and Lincoln orders a naval blockade of the Confederacy.

April 12, 1861 - First shot fired of the war.

April-May - Virginia, Arkansas, Tennessee and North Carolina secede and join the Confederacy.

June - First major battle fought at Manassas (Bull Run). A Confederate victory.

1862

February - Union forces under General Grant and Commodore Foote capture Forts Henry and Donelson and move into Western Tennessee.

February 6th - First Federal Naval victory

March - Federal victory at Pea Ridge (Elkhorn), Arkansas, Battle Between the Ironclads (Monitor and Merrimac) at Hampton Roads, Virginia.

April - U.S. Grant wins important victory at Shiloh and moves into Mississippi.
General McClellan opens Peninsular Campaign east of Richmond.
Stonewall Jackson begins Shenandoah Valley Campaign as a diversion of McClellan's troops.
New Orleans is occupied by Union forces.
General Joseph Johnston is wounded in the Battle of Seven Pines.

June - General Robert E. Lee replaces Johnston in command of the Army of Northern Virginia, fights the Seven Days Battles and drives McClellan away from Richmond.

July - Lee and Jackson win a second great victory at Manassas.

September - Lee's first invasion of Maryland; withdraws after defeat at Antietam (Sharpsburg).
Lincoln issues Emancipation Proclamation, to become effective January 1, 1863.

December - Lee defeats General Ambrose Burnside's forces at Fredericksburg.

December-January 1863 - Battle of Murfreesburo (Stone River).

1863

March - Congress authorizes Lincoln to suspend Right of Habeas Corpus.

March-July - Vicksburg Campaign.

April-May - Lee and Jackson win a great victory at Chancellorsville.
Jackson is mortally wounded.
General Nathan Bedford Forrest conducts brilliant campaign in Alabama.

June-July - Lee's second invasion of the north, defeat at Battle of Gettysburg.
Vicksburg falls to General Grant.
Union capture of Port Hudson gives the north complete control of Mississippi River.

September - General Braxton Bragg with General Forrest and General James Longstreet wins in the Battle of Chickamauga. Britain and France bar delivery of warships to the Confederacy.

November - The Union wins the Battle of Chattanooga, routing the Southerners to Georgia.
Lincoln gives the Gettysburg Address.

1864

January - General Forrest turns back a Union invasion of Mississippi.

March - General Forrest defeats Union forces holding Fort Pillow. Grant takes supreme command of all Union forces and launches drives by General George Meade in Virginia and General William Tecumseh Sherman in Georgia.

January-March - Sherman burns Columbia and moves into North Carolina leaving a path of devastation behind.

March - Final battles of Petersburg begin.
Confederacy approves military service for slaves.

April - General Lee surrenders the Confederate Army of Northern Virginia to General Grant at Appomattox Courthouse on April 9th.

On the aftermath of the war ...

April 14th, 1865 - President Lincoln is shot at Ford's Theatre in Washington during a performance of Our American Cousin by actor John Wilkes Booth. The President dies early the next morning, April 15. Andrew Johnson takes Oath of Office as President.

April - General Johnston surrenders the Army of Tennessee to General Sherman at Bennett Place near Durham Station, North Carolina.
Booth was assumed dead in a burning barn destroyed by Federal cavalry officers in Virginia.

May - Lee inflicts heavy losses on Union forces at the Wilderness, Spotsylvania Courthouse, and the North Anna River, but is forced south toward Richmond.
Sherman forces Johnston slowly back toward Atlanta.

June - Confederate raider ALABAMA sunk off Cherbourg, France, by U.S.S. KEARSARGE.
Lee defeats Grant at Cold Harbor. Both armies entrench south of Petersburg for a seige that lasts until April 1865.

August - General Forrest raids Memphis.
Battle of Mobile Bay.

September - Atlanta falls to Sherman.

November - President Lincoln re-elected for second term.
Battle of Franklin.
Sherman begins his infamous march from Atlanta to the sea.

December - End of Sherman's march to sea. Lower south removed from the war.
General Forrest attempts to help Hood save the army of Tennessee after defeat near Nashville.

1865

January - Union forces capture Fort Fisher and close the last Confederate Port at Wilmington.

May - Abraham Lincoln buried at Springfield, Illinois.
General Richard Taylor surrendered the Confederate forces of Alabama, Mississippi and Louisiana.
Jefferson Davis captured by Union forces in Georgia and imprisoned for two years in Fort Monroe, Virginia, awaiting a trial that was never held.
Last battle of the war, a Confederate victory, at Palmito Ranch, Brownsville, Texas.
Grand review of the Union armies for two days in Washington, the armies are disbanded.
The Confederate Army of the Trans-Mississippi surrenders at New Orleans.
General amnesty and paroles proclaimed by President Johnson.

DRAMATIS PERSONAE

The cast of characters in America's greatest drama, The Civil War, is headed by two outstanding individuals revered and beloved north and south of the Mason-Dixon Line, Abraham Lincoln and Robert E. Lee.

ABRAHAM LINCOLN was born into poverty in a frontier Kentucky cabin, February 12, 1809. He had no formal schooling; rather, he educated himself using the Bible and a small collection of books as learning tools. He became a lawyer and entered politics in Illinois. In time his backwoods wit and wisdom and brilliant gift of oratory catapulted him to the Republican Presidential Candidacy. He was not an abolitionist, but his rejection of slavery as cruel and unjust and his stand against it spread into free territories. Signaled the secession of seven southern states soon after his election in 1860.

As President of a nation at war with itself, Lincoln determined to restore the Union at all cost. With great political skill, patience and wisdom, he succeeded and even abolished slavery. But he did not live to carry out his humane and healing plans for reconstruction. He was assassinated by John Wilkes Boothe on April 14, 1865, five days after Lee's surrender at Appomattox Courthouse. He has been called The First American, and is regarded today as perhaps our greatest and most noble statesman, the embodiment of American democracy.

****

ROBERT E. LEE was born into the aristocratic Lee family of Virginia on January 19, 1807. His father, "Light-Horse Harry" Lee, was a Revolutionary War hero, a signer of the Declaration of Independence, and an early opponent of the slave-trade. By tradition, R.E. Lee was opposed to slavery and secession but he chose to fight for these causes, saying that he could not raise his sword against Virginia.

Lee was made Commander of the Army of Northern Virginia after the Battle of Seven Pines (June 1862) and in that capacity he became one of the greatest generals in world history. A southern Hannibal, his victories were stunning, and he made two audacious invasions of the north. He took personal blame for the Confederate defeat at Gettysburg, offering his resignation, which President Davis refused. He continued to hold the yankees back by his military genius, until at last men and supplies were exhausted.

His dignity, strength of character, courage and sense of fairness earned him the undying affection of his officers and his starving, ragged men who rallied about him after the surrender, shouting through their tears, "General, say the word and we'll go in and fight 'em yet!"

Though Congress ignored his request for a pardon (and indeed did not grant it until 1875), he worked after the war to restore the southern states to their place in the Union. Today he is remembered as a great American hero, a symbol of the American and Southern ideal.

****

It is emblematic of the "House Divided" that JEFFERSON DAVIS, the only President of the Confederate States of America, was also born in a log cabin in Kentucky. A slave-holding border state that remained in the Union. Davis was a West Point graduate, soldier and U.S. Senator who supported southern issues. When succession and war came he hoped to serve the south in some military capacity. He might have proven a great general early in the war, however, the Presidency was thrust upon him. Anguished by the enormity of the task, he nevertheless accepted it as his duty. Davis and his cabinet made many mistakes, some costly, some fatal, as they strove to create a new nation (the seeds of whose doom—states rights—were written into the Constitution) and wage a war with little or no central authority.

As hardships mounted and the Confederate sun began to set Davis was blamed for it's failure. He was the only one, however, who could not give up the dream, who refused to the last to admit defeat, and who when everything was in flames about him, set out to find a new capital and inspire the people to carry on with succession. Some thought him mad.

He was captured on the run, May 10, 1865, in Irwinsville, Georgia. Yankee newspapers accused him of disguising himself in women's clothing though it seems he only wore, as Lincoln had done, a shawl against the cold. They imprisoned him at Fort Monroe where for two years he was left to languish for a trial that was never held. Over the long years left to him he refused to ask for a pardon or ever to admit that secession or the war had been a mistake.

Toward the end of his life, Jefferson Davis, achieved the recognition of his fellow Americans as the courageous leader of a lost cause.

ULYSSES S. GRANT was the distinguished supreme commander of the Union armies during the Civil War. Dishevelled, hard-drinking, cigar-smoking, he was the antithesis of Lee's statuesque bearing and yet the two men were an even match in aggressive boldness, dogged determination and military genius. Grant was the victor of Murfreesboro, the architect of Vicksburg (some military historians call it the most outstanding maneuver of the war) and the savior of Chattanooga. Lincoln at last realized he was the man to drive the indefatigable Lee from the field and made his the second full general in U.S. history (Washington was first).

Grant at Appomattox is as legendary as Lee who was resplendent in a new full-dress uniform with jeweled saber and sash. Grant arrived late in muddy boots and a private's blouse; he wore no sword. He reminisced about the "old army" and the Mexican War until Lee had to remind him of the business at hand. Grant wrote out the terms of surrender in his own hand. Saying later he had no idea what he would write until he began. But the terms were magnanimous, even Lincolnesque: every officer and man could keep his own mule or horse, give his parole and go home if he would promise to wage war no more.

On the porch of the McLean house after the signing he saluted General Lee as did his staff officers. When his men began to shout, sing and fire off volleys in jubilation, he ordered a silence: "The war is over; the rebels are our countrymen again." He wished to spare them further humiliation.

****

Lee and Grant were both fortunate to have has as aides trusted and able lieutenants who could understand their grand strategies and carry out orders - contributing their own genius so that successes were sometimes greater than the original design encompassed. Lee lost his most valuable aide, Stonewall Jackson, in 1863. Military historians believe that Gettysburg might have turned out differently if Jackson, the brilliant tactician and master of the "Lightning Stroke", had been there to lead his second corps "Foot Cavalry."

****

The "Prayin'est General", STONEWALL JACKSON, gave God all the credit for his incredible feats at First Manassas (where his steadfastness earned him his nickname). The valley, Antietam, Second Manassas and Fredericksburg. He reached the peak of his career with the famous Flank March and Assault on the Union right at Chancellorsville, where he was mortally wounded by southern fire as he rode through the wilderness in the dark behind enemy lines. His arm was amputated and pneumonia set in. Before he died, Lee telegraphed: "You have lost your left arm; but I have lost my right arm." Lee was never able to replace Stonewall and though his Army of Northern Virginia went on to other victories, the dazzle of the incomparable Lee-Jackson combination was lost forever.

****

GENERAL WILLIAM TECUMSEH SHERMAN was Grant's mainstay. He grasped completely Grant's objective to destroy the south's war-making capability. When directed to get deep within enemy territory and inflict all the damage he could, Sherman set out on his infamous march from Atlanta to the sea. Like a plague his army descended on Georgia looting and living off the land, then burning and tearing up everything they could not use or carry off. From Savannah they turned north through the Carolinas. The rampage still inflames southern passions a century and more later. The tactic is terribly familiar today; we call it "Scorched Earth." But to Grant it was a superbly executed, essential complement to a two-way push (with his operations in Virginia) that would double-envelope a vastly weakened, dying Confederacy.

****

CONFEDERATES

Prominent among the Confederate generals were: ALBERT SIDNEY JOHNSTON, who bled to death at Shiloh; JOSEPH E. JOHNSTON, who won First Manassas, was wounded at Seven Pines and succeeded by Lee, defended Vicksburg and Atlanta. He was removed from the last post by President Davis, his "worst enemy" in the war; but Lee called on him to defend the Carolinas against Sherman. To whom he surrendered on April 26, 1865. He is said to have died from the cold he caught marching bareheaded years later at Sherman's funeral.

PIERRE G.T. BEAUREGUARD was second in command under Johnston at First Manassas and at the end in North Carolina. He also fired on Fort Sumter, and fought at Shiloh, Corinth and the defense of Charleston.

JAMES "OLD PETE" LONGSTREET led the right wing at Gettysburg, where he failed to follow Lee's order to attack at dawn on the second day. He was responsible for the victory at Chickamauga and led a brilliant attack at the wilderness. He surrendered with Lee at Appomattox.

BRAXTON BRAGG led the abortive invasion of Kentucky and lost the Battle of Chattanooga.

RICHARD EWELL succeeded Stonewall in command of the 2nd corps. His hesitation on the first day at Gettysburg cost the Confederates Cemetry Ridge. He lost a leg at Groveton and was captured at Saylor's Creek and imprisoned.

JOHN BELL HOOD lost a leg at Chickamauga and replaced Johnston in the defense of Atlanta. He was beaten by Sherman at Peachtree Creek, Ezra Church and Jonesboro leading to the fall of Atlanta. He was crippled at Franklin and shattered at Nashville.

A.P. HILL sported a beard as red as his battleshirt and with his fast marching "Light" Division proved a tower of strength to Lee and Jackson, who both called to him on their deathbeds. He was killed by a Union straggler in the last week of the war.

****

FEDERALS

The Union forces lacked competent leadership. The first of the generals to be replaced by President Lincoln was IRVIN McDOWELL soon after the humiliating Federal defeat at First Manassas. His job was given to GEORGE B. "LITTLE MAC" McCLELLAN, who though he was an extraordinarily capable organizer, never realized what a magnificent force he had created in the army of the Potomac or the depth and scope of the war to be fought. He was cautious to the point of timidity; Lincoln called it "the Slows".

McClellan lost three golden opportunities (at Yorktown, Seven Days and Antietam) to destroy the outnumbered Army of Northern Virginia. In exasperation Lincoln removed him and brought in JOHN POPE, from the western front.

Pope was insensitive and self-asserting. He infuriated his men by incessantly accusing them of cowardice. He earned the derision of friend and foe by issuing orders from "Headquarters in the Saddle." Lee observed, "Pope appears to have his headquarters where his hindquarters ought to be." His courtmartial of blameless GENERAL FITZ-HUGH PORTER after the Battle of Cedar Mountain is a further blot on his name.

It is better to speak of AMBROSE BURNSIDE'S "Bridge" (at Antietam Creek) or his uberous mutton-chop whiskers that inspired the Moniker "Sideburns" than to recall his gross incompetence at Fredericksburg where the lives of thousands of gallant Union soldiers were needlessly lost.

He was replaced by, "FIGHTING JOE" HOOKER, whose utterance "May God have mercy on General Lee, for I will have none." might better have been ... May God have mercy on the Army of the Potomac under my command, so badly was it used by him at Chancellorsville.

Other Union generals were HENRY "OLD BRAINS" HALLECK, relieved as General in Chief by Grant; EDWIN SUMNER, an elderly cavalry man, too old to learn "new tricks" as an infantry leader. DON CARLOS BUELL, out-maneuvered by Bragg, and then when he had Bragg at Perryville, let him get away. He was replaced by WILLIAM ROSECRANS who fled with his men from Chickamauga.

The most inefficient Union generals were BUTLER, BANKS, FREMONT, PATTERSON and SICKLES. Among the most successful leaders in blue were SHERIDAN, KEARNY, MEADE, SCHOFIELD, WILSON and GEORGE "THE ROCK OF CHICKAMAUGA" THOMAS. They were at times brilliant and heroic.

****

THE CAVALRIES

The Cavalries of the Confederacy are legendary for their razzle dazzle raids and daring generals. The most glamourous of all was J.E.B. "JEB" STUART, also known as "Beauty" Stuart for his luxuriant coiffure, red-lined cape and hat with waving ostrich plume. Others called him the "Last Cavalier" and "The Knight of the Golden Spurs" (he wore a pair of golden spurs sent to him by a feminine admirer in Baltimore.) Stuart used fancy dress to inspire the spirit of the chase in his troops who were outnumbered and outgunned by the Yankees. The prerequisite for joining a Confederate cavalry unit was owning a horse. Stuart's men were country lads bred in the saddle who could outride the northern city boys. Accomplished much in reconnaissance (Lee called them his "eyes and ears") but were criticized for the recklessness which led them to ignore or elaborate orders until they were virtually off on their own adventure, which could be costly to their cause (as at Gettysburg). Stuart was mortally wounded in 1864 at Yellow Tavern in a fight with Sheridan, whose brilliant star as a cavalry leader was just rising. From that time Confederate horse power waned.

Other great southern cavalry men were: FITZHUGH LEE, (R.E. Lee's nephew); WADE HAMPTON, of Hampton's Legion who led the "Beefsteak Raid" that rustled 2500 head of U.S. beef cattle for hungry Confederates; the legendary COLONEL JOHN MOSBY, whose territory behind the lines in northern Virginia was called "Mosby's Confederacy"; EARL VAN DORN, a great ladies' man killed not by a Union bullet but by a jealous southern husband; STAND WATIE, a Cherokee Indian from

Georgia who led the 1st Cherokee Mounted Rifles at Wilson's Creek, Elkhorn Tavern, and in other raids.

PHILIP SHERIDAN'S VI Corps swept the Shenadoah Valley clean of resistance and closed in on the Army of Northern Virginia at Five Forks, Amelia Courthouse and Saylor's Creek. GENERAL GEORGE CUSTER (later of Custer's last stand) served in these operations.

****

The most brilliant cavalry officer in the Confederacy was NATHAN BEDFORD FORREST, a man of no formal schooling but innate military genius, who is famous for his definition of strategy - "To git thar fust with the most men." He might have turned the war around if his talents had been sufficiently valued in Richmond; the Yankees never found a match for him. His supreme stroke was delivered at Brice's Crossroads. He also captured a Federal gunboat from the shore on horseback.

The boldest cavalry raids were accomplished by the dashing Kentuckian, JOHN HUNT MORGAN. He and his rough, capable horsemen extended the war to the peaceful farmlands of southern Indiana and Ohio. A popular song of the day, inspired by Morgan's actions was:
"I'm sent to warn the neighbors,
He's only a mile behind,
He's sweeping up the horses, every
horse he can find.
Morgan, Morgan, the Raider, and Morgan's
terrible men,
With bowie-knives and pistols,
are galloping up the glen.

But he failed as Jeff Davis' instrument of popular uprising in the border state of Kentucky.

Another group whose exploits live on in local legends was Coleman's Scouts. A Keystone Cop caper was pulled off by some Union soldiers called Andrews' Raiders. They stole the Confederate engine "The General" and led the rebels on a locomotive chase through Georgia. Andrews and seven of his men were hanged.

WILLIAM QUANTRILL does not deserve to be included in the list of outstanding Beaux-Sabreurs above. He was a cold-blooded killer who pillaged Kansas and the western front with the James brothers and Jim Younger in the guise of a Confederate officer. He was gunned down in Kentucky in 1865.

The last great cavalry actions of the war belonged to the Union horsemen, superior at last when the south had run out of horsemen and remounts. The engineer-cavalryman, GENERAL JAMES H. WILSON'S Selma Campaign has been called one of the most extraordinary in cavalry history. He mopped up the Confederacy from Muscle Shoals to Macon and captured Jefferson Davis.

FLAT-FOOTED SOLDIERS

The infantryman's day in camp on both sides began with the dreaded morning call, followed by hardtack, salt pork, coffee, drills, boredom and more drills. Camplife was brightened, however, by a camaraderie that few would ever enjoy again in civilian life. The men played basketball, boxed or engaged in such horseplay as "louse races". Their spirits were irrepressible and even foraging chickens and pigs from neighboring farms became a contest of wits. These escapades enlivened the tedious hours spent mending, washing, cooking, cleaning rifles and barbering. At night fellowship about the campfire where favorite songs were sung of sweethearts and mothers left behind brought on homesickness and longing.

Sometimes there were distinguished visitors to the camps. One wag tacked a sign on his tent in an encampment near Washington, "No Dogs or Senators Allowed Inside." There were sometimes parades for the dignitaries who came to look over the troops. General Lee told one such British notable to ignore the men's ragged breeches since "the enemy never sees the backs of my Texans."

FOUR-LEGGED SOLDIERS

Unsung heroes of the Civil War, horses and mules were the backbone of hauling and indispensable for cavalry and artillery. They were often hungry and overworked, sick, wounded or killed. At the beginning of the war the south had the advantage in blood horses and brilliant riders (boys were brought up in the saddle in the rural southland), but as the wearing years rolled on, the Confederacy could no longer replace it's horses and mules, and the Union caught up and surpassed them in skills and supplies. Finding forage for horses and mules was always a challenge in the south. But when men became desperately hungry (as in Vicksburg in July 1863) they ate mule meat.

General Nathan Forrest was said to have killed 30 men in hand to hand combat and had 29 horses shot from under him. He was "a horse ahead" at the end. A yankee prisoner of Mosby's Rangers made a successful getaway on the "Gray Ghost's" own horse.

In a raid on federal stables at Lexington, Kentucky, in 1864, General John H. Morgan stole 7000 horses for the Confederacy.

The most famous horse in the Civil War was Lee's TRAVELLER, an iron grey steed, sixteen hands with black mane and tail who never shied under fire but once and the cannonball passed harmlessly under his rearing legs.

Also, well-known was Stonewall Jackson's LITTLE SORREL, a short, thick gelding captured from the Yankees, who could go without water like a camel and lived contentedly on corncobs.

And then there was RIENZI, the immortal jet-black morgan horse who carried his master, Union cavalry General Philip Sheridan, over 20 miles at a gallop on his famous ride to turn back panic-stricken, fleeing troops to defeat Jubal Early at Cedar Creek. Thomas Read wrote the schoolboy's favorite poem, "Sheridan's Ride" several days after the event and made Rienzi's name legendary for half a century.

****

WOMEN AND THE WAR

Many women followed their husbands' regiments, nursing the wounded throughout the war. Others rushed to aid the wounded and dying after every major battle, some going onto the battlefields and rescuing those left for dead. Though suffrage and equality were far in the future, women emerged on both sides to play important roles in the national crisis. Here briefly are some of the most remarkable.

CLARA BARTON who later founded The American Red Cross, resigned her patent office job at the outbreak of war and set up a soldier's supply service. As casualties mounted she turned to nursing and became known as the "Angel of the Battlefield". In 1865 Lincoln asked her to search for missing prisoners and her records helped identify thousands of the dead at Andersonville Prison.

BELLE BOYD was the most romantic and sensational of the Confederacy's lady spies. She passed many Union secrets to "Jeb" Stuart, Beauregard and Stonewall Jackson from her Washington social connections. Stonewall awarded her a captain's commission and made her an honorary aide-de-camp.

ANNA ELLA CARROLL, a political writer, came to Lincoln's attention with her pamphlet on The Powers of the Presidency During Wartime. He sent her on a fact-finding mission to the Western Front, where she observed stalemated operations on the Mississippi River and formulated a plan for an offensive campaign on the Cumberland and Tennessee Rivers which later became effective Union strategy.

DOROTHEA DIX, already well known as a pioneer in reform of insane asylums, volunteered to organize women for nursing at the war's outset. The War Department appointed her superintendent of the First Army Corps of Nurses.

ANNIE ETHERIDGE served throughout the war as a battlefront nurse and was awarded the Kearny Cross, given in all others instances to enlisted men for valor on the battlefield.

ROSE GREENHOW was the widow of a prominent Washingtonian who gathered information of Union troop strength and positions and passed it in coded messages to General Beauregard, who used it to advantage in the Battle of First Manassas. She was imprisoned and branded a "dangerous" spy.

SARAH and ANGELINA GRIMKE were socially prominent South Carolinian sisters who had become Quakers and gone north to speak out for women's rights and the abolition of slavery before the war. They continued their work during the war, and afterwards when they learned they were aunts to two black nephews by their brother and a former slave woman, they opened their hearts and homes to the boys, and helped with their educations. One nephew, Archibald Grimke became a distinguished crusader for negro advancement.

JULIA WARD HOWE was a social reformer and humanitarian who worked throughout her life for the abolition of slavery, women's suffrage and world peace. Her great war contribution was the words to "The Battle Hymn of the Republic" which glow with her spirit of Yankee Puritan fervor.

HARRIET BEECHER STOWE was - in Lincoln's words - "the little woman who made the great big war." Her incredibly popular novel Uncle Tom's Cabin, in which she described slavery for good or evil as she had witnessed it in Kentucky, galvanized Northern, and world opinion against slave-holding. Queen Victoria was an avid fan of Mrs. Stowe.

SALLY TOMPKINS worked tirelessly among the wounded in Richmond during four years of war. She was made a captain in the Confederate Army and offered a commendation but she refused to let her name be listed on the payroll.

SOJOURNER TRUTH was a former slave and a religious mystic whose heavenly voices called her away from domestic work and out into the world as a dynamic speaker for the rights of negroes and women. She was a lifetime illiterate but a forceful personality who worked ceasely for her causes.

HARRIET TUBMAN was called "Moses" because she led at least 300 of her people out of bondage and into the promised land of freedom. She was the most famous "conductor" on the underground railroad. Having made her own escape from slavery as a young woman, guiding herself across the country at night by the North Star. She went back south many times though there was a price on her head and brought out large groups of slaves, including her own aged parents. If any one faltered from fear or weariness and thought to turn back, Harriet held a pistol to his head and threatened freedom or death. During the war she attached herself to Union forces and made many trips behind the lines as a spy and guide for "contraband" slaves. She knew famous people such as John Brown, the Alcotts and the Howes, and lived to be a very old woman.

****

NEGROES DURING THE WAR YEARS

"... on the first day of January, in the year of our Lord one thousand eight hundred and sixty-three, all persons held as slaves within any state, or designated part of a state, the people whereof shall then be in rebellion against the United States, shall be then, thenceforward, and forever free; and the executive government of the United States, including the military and naval authority thereof, will recognize and maintain the freedom of such persons, and will do no act or acts to repress such persons, or any of them, in any efforts they may make for their actual freedom...."

—Abraham Lincoln
The Emancipation Proclamation

The primary goal of the Civil War was not the abolition of slavery, though fiery abolitionists demanded it. The North's main objective was to restore to the Union the states which had seceeded. It is probable that if "the rebellion" had been quashed in the first few battles, the southern states could have returned to the Union with slavery still an issue to be decided by each state. But the longer the war continued, the more it became clear to the people of the North that the Confederacy would have to be totally destroyed and with it, the "peculiar institution" of slavery.

Refugees of slavery streamed behind every Union army. They were housed in enormous camps. Eventually the men were given guns and uniforms and enlisted to do their part in fighting for their freedom. A man who served his country in it's armed forces need never go back to being a second class citizen. Lincoln knew this and drew up a document to free all of the slaves, however, he needed a Federal victory to give the words authority. This came about when McClellan's army turned back Lee's first invasion of Maryland at Antietam, September 1862, and at this time Lincoln read his Emancipation Proclamation, though it would not take effect until January 1, 1863, and even then would not free any slave in Confederate Territory. Slavery was finished from that day forward, not by any official proclamation, but by the sweeping social changes which total war wrought. The restored Union would be a different nation. Never again in the United States could one human being be the property of another.

****

General Robert E. Lee was not an advocate of slavery. His wife, Mary, inherited slaves from her father, George W. Parke Custin (the grandson of Martha Washington), who died in 1857 and by this will the slaves were to be manumitted. Lee effected the Manumission December 29, 1862. He wrote to his son Curtis that being a slave-owner was "an unpleasant legacy."

****

"From east to west, from north to south, the sky is written all over, — Now or Never. Liberty won by white men would lose half it's luster, who would be free, themselves must strike the blow. Better even die free, than to live slaves..."

—Frederick Douglass, 1863

****

The sons of Frederick Douglass, Charles and Lewis Douglass, served with the 54th Massachusetts Colored Regiment which charged Fort Wagner, South Carolina, July 18, 1863.

****

The abolitionist general, Ben Butler, used negro troops extensively since "I knew they would fight more desperately than any white troops, in order to prevent capture, because they knew if they were captured they would be returned to slavery."

****

The first negro field officer to serve in the Civil War was Major Martin R. Delany of the 194th Regiment at Charleston, a Harvard Medical School graduate.

****

The first major battle in which negro troops took part was the capture of Port Hudson, Louisiana, on May 27, 1863.

****

A negro soldier took his former master prisoner at the Battle of Milliken's Bend, June 6, 1863.

****

Nathan Bedford Forrest's Cavalry was charged with atrocities and massacre of negro soldiers at Fort Pillow, Tennessee, April 12, 1864. The charges were vehemently denied at hearings after the event, and reliable evidence was difficult to produce.

****

In July 1863, in New York City, mobs turned on negro citizens for causing the war during draft riots that raged for four days. A negro orphanage was burned, as were shops and homes owned by black people.

****

Planter, a Confederate gunboat was stolen by it's slave crew while white officers slept ashore in Charleston in the spring of 1862. One black seaman managed to smuggle his family aboard before steaming out to the Union blockade vessels where he hoisted a white flag and presented the gunboat as a gift from the Confederacy. Congress later awarded this seaman, Robert Smalls, a sum for the contraband ship.

****

There were negro seamen aboard the ironclad Monitor and one-fourth of all Union sailors were black. Four negroes won the Navy's Medal of Honor.

****

In the last days of the war, the South prepared to jetison slavery in the hopes of bringing in England at last. One of the final acts of the Confederate Congress, in March 1865, was to make it legal for slaves to join the army as soldiers bearing arms. It came much too late to help the lost cause.

****

NAVAL HIGHLIGHTS OF THE WAR

At the outset neither side was prepared to wage war at sea. The barely adequate U.S. Fleet was scattered around the world or out of commission; the Confederate Navy was non-existent. The Southerners, never sea-faring, had few ships of any sort, fewer harbors, and no ship-building industry. Their only naval yard, Norfolk, had been heavily damaged by departing Federal officers after Virginia seceded. Both sides, however, rallied with great ingenuity to the work at hand and necessity was often the mother of bold invention. The Civil War, it's outcome largely determined at sea and on inland waters, ushered in the modern age of American sea power.

****

ALABAMA was the most notorious southern commerce raider, under ruthless Captain Raphael Semmes, the British-built steam powered schooner destroyed 58 Federal vessels during her two year prowl. She was sunk June 19, 1864, off Cherbourg, France, in a broadside duel with the U.S.S. Kearsarge. Captain Semmes jumped overboard and was rescued by an English yacht.

****

ALBEMARLE, a formidable Confederate ironclad ram, was built of scrounged scrap in the Roanoke River, far from any shipyard, by Commander J.W. Cooke. Two days after her commission in April 1864 she sank the U.S.S. Smithfield, and forced three other Federal vessels to withdraw, yielding the Port of Plymouth, North Carolina to the Confederates. She was sunk in the darkness of October 27, 1864, eight miles up the Roanoke by a Federal torpedo ship, fitted out for the task by the daring young Lt. William B. Cushing, U.S.N.

****

BLOCKADE, of all southern seaports was proclaimed by President Lincoln after the fall of Fort Sumter. He immediately realized the political blunder of this proclamation. A nation with internal strife "closes it's ports." A nation at war with another nation imposes a blockade. Thus, the blockade conferred instant independent status upon the Confederacy, which foreign powers promptly recognized, with amusement at Lincoln's backwoods ignorance. Then, too, it could not be a "paper blockade"; the ships to enforce it had to be on station outside each southern port or it would have no legal standing in international law. Secretary of the Navy Gideon Welles rose to the challenge and quickly rounded up an armada of whalers, tugboats, racing yachts, ferryboats, excursion steamers, fishing schooners and clipperships which made the blockade legally effective until the navy could build a fleet of "ninety-day wonder" gunboats.

****

SOUTHERN, BLOCKADE-RUNNERS immediately began to slip past Welles' curious flotilla and later the Union warships that lay offshore from Chesapeake Bay to Galveston. There was some risk involved for the low, fast, fog-colored ships that burned smokeless coal and darted out from the coastlines in darkness and foul weather. But many were eager to take the risk because two runs to Nassau or Europe with a hold full of cotton and back again with guns, ammunitions and luxury goods would pay for the ship and the cargo. Indeed the trade in "watered silk and geegaws" was so profitable that, as the blockade tightened, the Confederate Congress passed a law that only necessities could be brought in.

It has been estimated that 1,650 runners made 8,000 round trips through the blockade. One of the most successful was the side-wheeler Nashville, which slipped through repeatedly with tons of munitions for Confederate Armies. Rebel ironclads shelled and rammed blockaders, but in the end all attempts to end the blockade failed and the Confederacy was defeated.

****

CHARLESTON, was the Confederacy's most strategic port, as well as the birthplace of secession and the site of the first shot fired in the war on Fort Sumter. For these reasons the Union tried to take the city by siege, bombardment and blockade. On April 7, 1863, Union soldiers managed to reduce Fort Sumter to rubble but still the fortress held. Charleston was a proud Confederate stronghold until February, 1865, when Sherman cut it off by land.

ADMIRAL DAVID FARRAGUT, U.S.N., led his powerful fleet past heavy bombardment at the narrow entrance of Mobile Bay before dawn on August 5, 1864. When the decks of his flagship, Hartford, became slippery with blood he climbed into the rigging to command the action. By first light Farragut saw the bay was studded with mines (historically called torpedoes). "Damn the torpedoes! Full speed ahead!" he cried, determined to take the blockade - Running Haven. At close range Hartford battled furiously with the Confederate ironclad, Tennessee, commanded by the pre-war superintendent of Annapolis, Franklin Buchannan. By mid-morning "Old Buck", outnumbered and badly damaged, was forced to surrender the southern stronghold of Mobile Bay.

****

FORT FISHER, guarded the entrance to the Cape Fear River and Wilmington, N.C., the last Confederate refuge of blockage-runners who brought in supplies carried by the Wilmington and Weldon Railroad to Lee's forges. In late 1864 the Union sent a land-sea force against Fort Fisher under General Benjamin Butler and Admiral David Porter. Butler attacked and then faintheartedly withdrew. He was replaced by General Alfred Terry. Lee telegraphed Fort Fisher to hold or else Richmond must be evacuated. The earthenwork fortification held out for three days, but fell on January 15, 1865, closing the South's last door to the outside world.

****

CSS H.L. HUNLEY was an experimental submarine designed for the Confederate Navy by Horace Hunley who perished in it's trial run. The cigar shaped "semi-submersible" scored history's first submaring victory when it sunk the U.S.S. Housatonic, off Charleston on February 17, 1864. Lt. George Dixon and the six man crew of the Hunley, died in the victim's explosion.

****

The first IRONCLAD was built by the French in 1859 but the Union and Confederate Navies during the Civil War pioneered and developed the strange craft that were the fore-runners of modern steel ships. Wooden warships became obsolete when the ironclads were born.

****

The most famous ironclads were the USS MONITOR and CSS VIRGINIA, which had been the old USS Merrimack. A steam powered sailing frigate scuttled when the U.S. Navy departed Norfolk in 1861. The Confederates raised, overhauled and armored her with flattened railroad track, a sensational achievement. In her first spectacular day of action she destroyed three U.S. ships. The very next day, March 9, 1862, however, she met the Union's "Tin Can on a Shingle," the ironclad Monitor, in Hampton Roads. The famous four hour battle was a stand off. Virginia sank no more U.S. ships but her presence in the James River slowed McClellan's peninsular campaign. She was sunk by her own crew when the Confederates evacuated Norfolk.

****

ADMIRAL DAVID PORTER, U.S.N., served brilliantly in the New Orleans and Vicksburg campaigns and in the siege of Fort Fisher. His most incredible feat was accomplished at Alexandria, Louisiana in May 1864, when his shallow draught Mississippi squadron of gunboats were stranded in the Red River through the ineptitude of General Banks. Rather than scuttle the two million dollar fleet, Admiral Porter decided to try the ingenious plan of a young naval engineer and build wingdams to raise the water level. The Herculean task was accomplished in 10 days, causing the river to rise and the ships to float downstream to safety.

PRIVATEERING, the practice of privately owned armed vessels operating against enemy trading during wartime which had flourished during the revolution and the War of 1812, waned during the Civil War, both sides preferred to arm merchantmen as warships than to commission privateers. The Confederate schooner, Savannah, was the most famous privateer of the Civil War. When it's men were taken prisoners they were charged with piracy, a capitol crime. President Davis sent a letter to President Lincoln advising him that 32 high-ranking Union prisoners from Manassas would be chosen by lots to hang for any executed members of the Savannah's crew. This caused Lincoln to declare that all captured privateers would thereafter be treated as prisoners of war.

****

SHENANDOAH, was a Confederate commerce raider that single-handedly did much to destroy the Yankee whaling industry, burning 25 whalers of the Arctic Fleet in one week in the Bering Sea — two months after the war ended. When the Shenandoah's captain was informed that the war was over in August 1865, he stowed his guns and sailed for Liverpool, where he surrendered to British authorities on November 6th.

****

THE TRENT AFFAIR, was a diplomatic incident in which the U.S. Navy forcibly removed two Confederate commissioners, James Mason and John Slidell, from the British Mail Packet, Trent, against International Law of the Sea. The Southerners were taken aboard the U.S. warship San Jacinto, and brought to prison in Boston. Britain protested strongly and it seemed that Britain would come to the aid of the Confederacy along with Canada, however, international war was averted when the men were released in January of 1862.

****

See pages 26 and 27 for centerfold map of the battles of the Civil War and map key.

MEDICAL CARE

Though Civil War statistics are not too reliable, it is generally accepted that about 1,500,000 men fought in Union armies and 1,000,000 in the Confederate forces. Approximately 617,000 lost their lives, 359,000 Union and 258,000 Confederate. It is also estimated that for every one of these deaths from battlewounds three men died of disease. The diseases that took the heaviest toll were Dysentery, Typhoid, Typhus, Smallpox, Measles, Malaria and other "camp fevers". No one knew what caused these diseases; sanitation and hygiene were infant sciences, so that camplife was more dangerous to a soldier than battle.

However, both sides tried to provide adequate medical care for those wounded in battle. What was adequate then does not compare to present day standards. Medical arts had not emerged from the dark ages while military science had advanced to deadly modern efficiency and accuracy.

A soldier was likely to be critically mutilated if wounded. For instance, the widely used, French designed minnie ball was an enormous bullet with a diameter of .69 of an inch. Most battle wounds required radical surgery - amputation. The wounded, who may have lain for as long as two days in rain, cold or heat on the field, were carried by jolting, horse-drawn ambulances to inadequately staffed field hospitals. Many did not survive the trip. After surgery (in which doctors' hands and instruments were rarely clean, let alone sterile), unsterile bandages made of lint (which most American women were busy making) were applied. These lint bandages promoted infection.

One modern historian has noted, in fact, that few Civil War generals could pass a modern physical.

****

Map of the Battleg

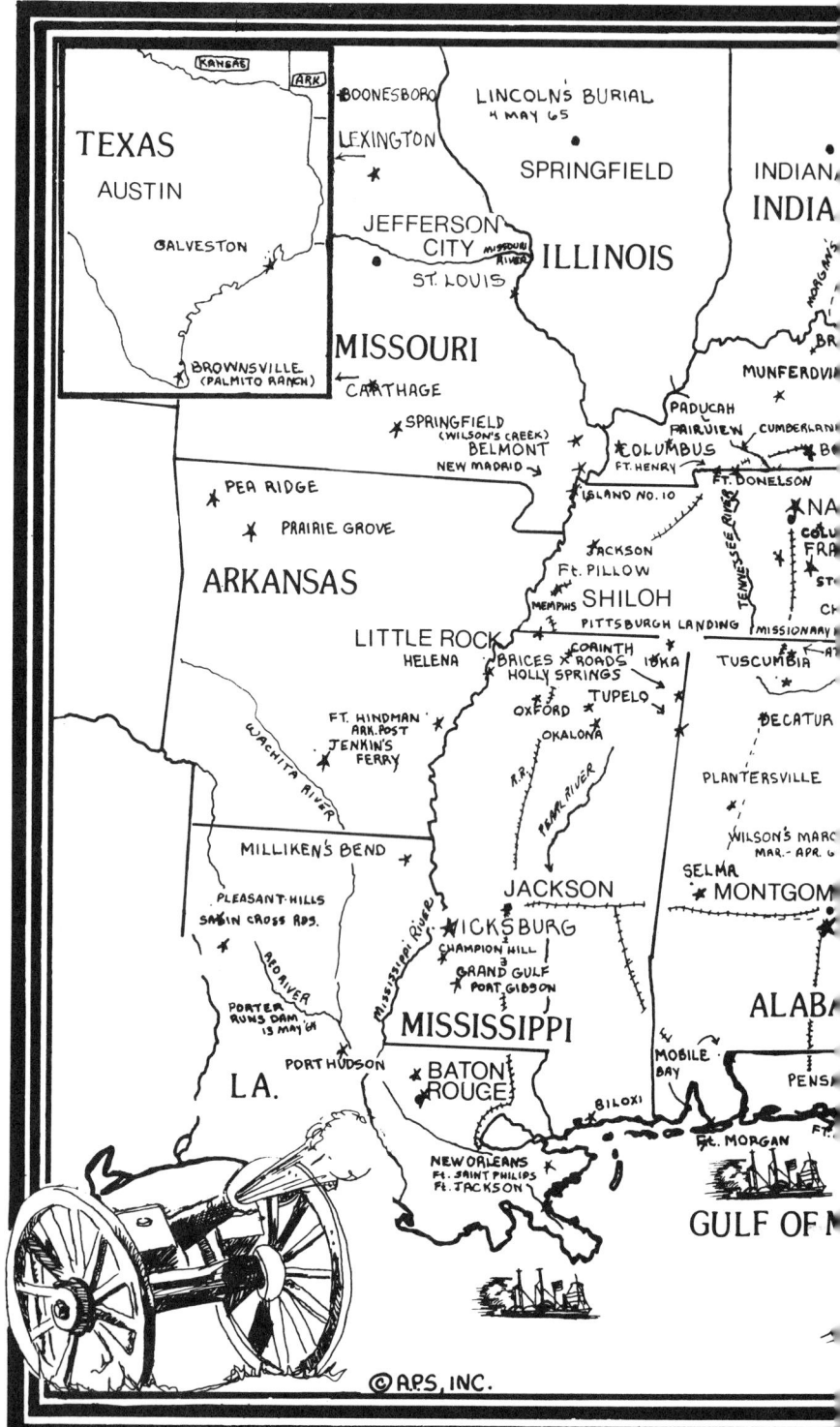

s of the Civil War

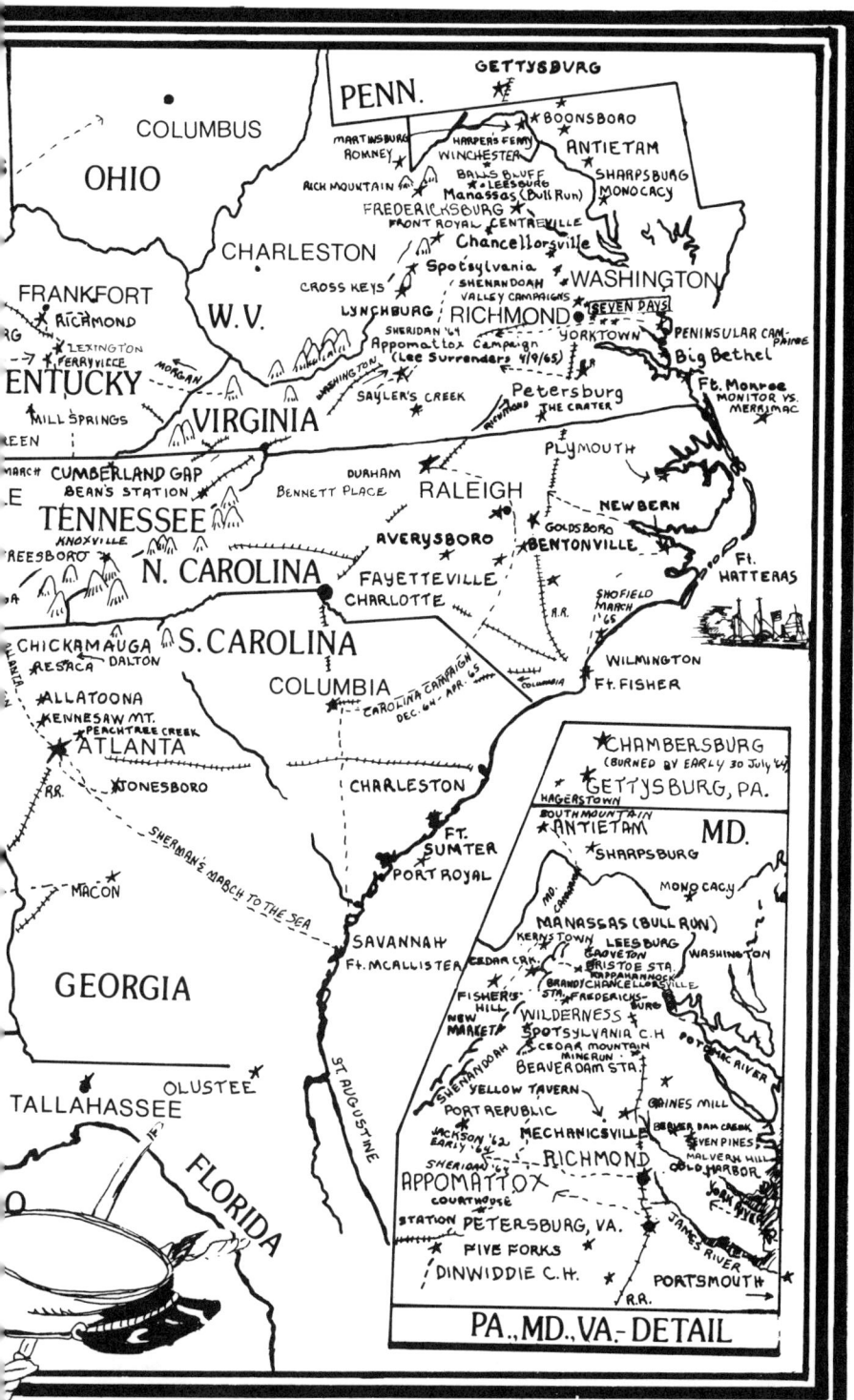

CIVIL WAR PRISONS

"Better dead than captured by Johnny Reb", was a popular saying among Union soldiers as conditions in Confederate prisons, such as Libby and Belle Island, became known. Andersonville, a prison camp in the Georgia Pine Barrens, became synonymous with all that is cruel and inhumane in the treatment of prisoners of war.

Camp Douglas was equally as bad and could not be excused by general hardships as in the South. Statistics show that from among 220,000 Confederates in northern prisons . . . 26,000 died and of 127,000 imprisoned Union soldiers . . . 22,500 died. The Union captive death rate is a lower figure but a higher percentage. It was estimated that one Yankee died every 11 minutes at Andersonville.

Prisoner exchange — a general for a general, a private for a private — eventually broke down over the question of returning negro soldiers who had been run-away slaves, and southern prisoners who would almost immediately be returned to combat. Knowing that the South could not long bear the loss of manpower, Grant cancelled the paroles, thus, northern soldiers were left to languish in southern prisons until the cessation of hostilites or death.

****

PROSE, POETRY AND SONGS OF THE CIVIL WAR

THE GETTYSBURG ADDRESS

On November 19, 1863, Abraham Lincoln took the train from Washington to Pennsylvania to help dedicate the National Soldiers' Cemetery on the battlefield at Gettysburg. Thousands of people attended the ceremony. Prayers and band music were followed by Edward Everett's two hour oration. Then Lincoln gave the five minute address he had written on the train. Many people could not hear him. Applause was polite but less enthusiastic than for Everett. Lincoln felt his words had fallen flat. Only a few in the audience realized they had heard one of the greatest speeches of all time. When the ten sentences were published, they began to be recognized as the most eloquent and moving statement of the American Creed and an immortal literary achievement.

Four score and seven years ago our fathers brought forth, on this continent, a new nation, conceived in liberty, and dedicated to the proposition that all men are created equal.

Now we are engaged in a great Civil War, testing whether that nation, or any nation so conceived and so dedicated, can long endure. We are met here on a great battlefield of that war. We have come to dedicate a portion of that field as a final resting place for those who here gave their lives that that nation might live. It is altogether fitting and proper that we should do this.

But, in a larger sense, we can not dedicate — we can not consecrate — we can not hallow — this ground. The brave men, living and dead, who struggled here, have consecrated it, far above our poor power to add or detract. The world will little note, nor long remember what we say here, but it can never forget what they did here. It is for us the living, rather, to be dedicated here to the unfinished work which they who fought here have thus far so nobly advanced. It is rather for us to be here dedicated to the great task remaining before us — that from these honored dead we take increased devotion to that cause for which they gave the last full measure of devotion — that we here highly resolve that these dead shall not have died in vain — that this nation under God, shall have a new birth of freedom — and that government of the people, by the people, for the people, shall not perish from the earth.

— Abraham Lincoln

LEE'S FAREWELL TO HIS ARMY

When General Lee mounted his horse, Traveller, and prepared to ride away from the McClean house in Appomattox Courthouse, Virginia, after signing the surrender papers with General Ulysses S. Grant, he was saluted by Grant and by the Union officers in the yard. They all knew Lee to be a brilliant leader and an honorable and even noble adversary. As he rode back among them, his own weeping men cheered him, but he told them his heart was too full to speak more than briefly. That night he had an aid, Charles Marshall, draw up "An Order to the Troops." The next morning Lee briefly edited and made a few changes to the text of "Gen'l Order, Number 9" which he signed and sent to his staff and corps commanders. It was instantly recognized and one of the great documents of American history.

Headquarters, Army of Northern Virginia
April 10th, 1865

After four years of arduous service, marked by unsurpassed courage and fortitude, the Army of Northern Virginia has been compelled to yield to overwhelming numbers and resources. I need not tell the survivors of so many hard-fought battles, who have remained steadfast to the last, that I have consented to this result from no distrust of them, but feeling that valor and devotion could accomplish nothing that could compensate for the loss that would have attended the continuation of the contest. I have determined to avoid the useless sacrifice of those whose past service have endeared them to their countrymen.

By the terms of the agreement, officers and men can return to their homes, and remain there until exchanged. You will take with you the satisfaction that proceeds from the consciousness of duty faithfully performed, and I earnestly pray that a merciful God will extend to you his blessings and protection.

With an unceasing admiration of your constancy and devotion to your country, and a grateful remembrance of your kind and generous consideration of myself, I bid you an affectionate farewell.

— R.E. Lee, General

BARBARA FRIETCHIE

It is true that Stonewall Jackson led a column of men into Frederick, Maryland, in September 1862. The rest is an irresistable blend of fact and fiction, producing a legend so appealing it overshadows the authenticated histories. When the Yankee poet, John Greenleaf Whittier, heard the story of Frederick's Fiesty None-Genarian. He immortalized her in one of America's best-loved poems, thus proving that the pen was mightier than the gleaming swords of that autumn day.

Up from the meadows rich with corn,
Clear in the cool September morn,

The clustered spires of Frederick stand
Green-walled by the hills of Maryland.

Round about them orchards sweep,
Apple and peach trees fruited deep,

Fair as the garden of the Lord
To the eyes of the famished rebel horde,

On that pleasant morn of the early fall
When Lee marched over the mountain-wall;

Over the mountain winding down,
Horse and foot, into Frederick town.

Forty flags with their silver stars,
Forty flags with their crimson bars,

Flapped in the morning winds, the sun
Of noon looked down, and saw not one.

Up rose old Barbara Frietchie then,
Bowed with her four score years and ten;

Bravest of all in Frederick town,
She took up the flag the men hauled down;

In her attic window the staff she set,
To show that one heart was loyal yet.

Up the street came the rebel tread,
Stonewall Jackson riding ahead.

Under his slouched hat left and right
He glanced, the old flag met his sight.

"Halt!" - the dust-brown ranks stood fast,
"Fire!" - out blazed the rifle-blast.

It shivered the window, pane and sash;
It rent the banner with seam and gash.

Quick, as it fell, from the broken staff
Dame Barbara snatched the silken scarf.

She leaned far out on the window sill,
And shook it forth with a royal will.

"Shoot, if you must, this old gray head,
But spare your country's flag," she said.

A shadow of sadness, a blush of shame,
Over the face of the leader came;

The nobler nature within him stirred
To life, at that woman's deed and word;

"Who touches a hair on yon gray head
Dies like a dog! March on!" he said.

All the day long that free flag tost
Over the heads of the rebel host.

Ever it's torn folds rose and fell
On the loyal winds that loved it well;

And through the hill-gaps sunset light
Shone over it with a warm goodnight.

Barbara Frietchie's work is o'er,
And the rebel rides on his raids no more.

Honor to her, and let a tear
Fall, for her sake on Stonewall's bier.

Over Barbara Frietchie's grave,
Flag of freedom and union, wave!

Peace and order and beauty draw
Round thy symbol of light and law;

And ever the stars above look down
On the stars below in Frederick town!

— John Greenleaf Whittier

O CAPTAIN! MY CAPTAIN!

The body of the murdered Lincoln lay in state in the Capitol Rotunda for two days following a funeral service in the White House April 19, 1865. The slain president had just been elected to his second term, witnessed the successful end of the long and bloody Civil War, and restored his beloved sundered Union. His greatest goals had been achieved, but satisfaction in his achievements was stopped by an assassin's bullet. As his funeral train wound it's slow way from Washington to New York to his final resting place in Springfield, Illinois, hundreds of thousands of mourning Americans along the courtege route bowed hatless heads, or held out flowers to the passing car. Most wept unashamedly. At night bonfires lit the darkness along the way. One citizen, Walt Whitman the poet, wrote two poems to express his sorrow and they have become the best known of all he wrote, "When Lilacs Last in the Dooryard Bloom'd" and the even more widely read "O Captain! My Captain!"

O Captain! My Captain! Our fearful trip is done,
The ship was weathered every rack, the prize we sought is won,
The port is near, the bells I hear, the people all exulting,
While follow eyes the steady keel, the vessel grim and daring;
       But O heart! Heart! Heart!
       O the bleeding drops of red,
       Where on the deck my Captain lies
       Fallen cold and dead.

O Captain! My Captain! Rise up and hear the bells;
Rise up — for you the flag is flung — for you the bugle trills,
For you the bouquets and ribboned wreaths —
 for you the shores a-crowding,
For you they call, the swaying mass, their eager faces turning;

Here Captain! Dear Father!
This arm beneath your head!
It is some dream that on the deck,
You've fallen cold and dead.

My Captain does not answer, his lips are pale and still,
My father does not feel my arm, he has no pulse not will,
The ship is anchored safe and sound, it's voyage closed and done,
From fearful trip the victor ship comes in with object won:

Exult O shores, and ring O bells!
But I with mournful tread,
Walk the deck my Captain lies,
Fallen cold and dead.

— Walt Whitman

THE BLUE AND THE GRAY

This sentimental poem, written by Francis Miles Finch in 1867, was inspired by women in Columbus, Mississippi, who placed flowers on the graves of both Confederate and Union dead. It was often read on Memorial Day, a holiday previously called Decoration Day, which was inaugurated in 1868 by General John A. Logan to decorate the graves of Civil War veterans.

By the flow of the inland river,
Whence the fleets of iron have fled,
Where the blades of the grave-grass quiver,
Asleep are the ranks of the dead:
Under the sod and the dew,
Waiting the Judgement Day —
Under the one, the Blue;
Under the other, the Gray.

These in the robings of glory,
Those in the gloom of defeat,
All with the battle-blood gory,
In the dusk of eternity meet:
Under the sod and the dew,
Waiting the Judgement Day —
Under the Laurel, the Blue;
Under the Willow, the Gray.

From the silence of sorrowful hours,
The desolate mourners go,
Lovingly laden with flowers,
Alike for the friend and foe:
Under the sod and the dew,
Waiting the Judgement Day —
Under the Roses, the Blue;
Under the Lilacs, the Gray.

So, with an equal splendor,
The morning sunrays fall,
With a touch impartially tender,
On the blossoms blooming for all:
Under the sod and the dew,
Waiting the Judgement Day —
Broidered with Gold, the Blue;
Mellowed with Gold, the Gray.

So, when the summer calleth,
On forest and field of grain,
With an equal murmur falleth
The cooling drip of the rain:
Under the sod and the dew,
Waiting the Judgement Day —
Wet with the rain, the Blue;
Wet with the rain, the Gray.

Sadly, but not with upbraiding,
The generous deed was done,
In the storm of the years that are fading
No braver battle was won:
Under the sod and the dew,
Waiting the Judgement Day —
Under the Blossoms, the Blue;
Under the Garlands, the Gray.

No more shall the war cry sever,
Or the winding rivers be red:
They banish our anger forever
When they Laurel the graves of our dead!
Under the sod and the dew,
Waiting the Judgement Day —
Love and tears for the Blue;
Tears and love for the Gray.

— Francis Miles Finch

THE LEGEND OF JOHN BROWN

On a rainy October night in 1859, John Brown, a fiery Kansas abolitionist, led a handful of followers in a surprise attack on the U.S. Arsenal at Harper's Ferry, Virginia. Even at that early date, Brown envisioned his raid as the first blow in an all out war for the liberation of the slaves.

John Brown's adament opposition to human bondage and vehement self-righteousness (which some saw as madness) made him a pivotal character and catalyst in the opening chapter of the Civil War.

Soon after the outbreak of war, a Boston regiment began to sing about the hanged crusader to William Steffe's well-known camp tune. It became popular throughout the Union ranks and later the same tune inspired the words of "The Battle Hymn of the Republic".

John Brown's Body

John Brown's body lies a-mouldering in the grave,
John Brown's body lies a-mouldering in the grave,
John Brown's body lies a-mouldering in the grave,
His soul is marching on.

Chorus Glory! Glory hallelujah!
Glory! Glory hallelujah!
Glory! Glory hallelujah!
His soul is marching on.

The stars of heaven are looking kindly down,
The stars of heaven are looking kindly down,
The stars of heaven are looking kindly down,
On the grave of old John Brown.

Chorus Repeat as above

He's gone to be a soldier in the Army of the Lord,
He's gone to be a soldier in the Army of the Lord,
He's gone to be a soldier in the Army of the Lord,
His soul is marching on.

Chorus Repeat as above

John Brown's knapsack is strapp'd upon his back,
John Brown's knapsack is strapp'd upon his back,
John Brown's knapsack is strapp'd upon his back,
His soul is marching on.

Chorus Repeat as above

His pet lambs will meet him on the way,
His pet lambs will meet him on the way,
His pet lambs will meet him on the way,
And they'll go marching on.

Chorus Repeat

We'll hang Jeff Davis on a sour apple tree,
We'll hang Jeff Davis on a sour apple tree,
We'll hang Jeff Davis on a sour apple tree,
As we go marching on.

Chorus Repeat and Finish

THE BATTLE HYMN OF THE REPUBLIC

When Julia Ward Howe heard Union troops singing "John Brown's Body" in December 1861, she went back to her Washington hotel room determined to write some more dignified words to go with William Steffe's stirring music. When people read the words, published in the Atlantic Monthly, February 1862, they began to sing them and "The Battle Hymn of the Republic" soon became one of the nation's most renowned songs.

        Mine eyes have seen the glory of the coming of the Lord;
        He is trampling out the vintage where the grapes of wrath
          are stored;
        He has loosed the fateful lightning of his terrible swift sword;
        His truth is marching on.

Chorus Glory! Glory hallelujah! Glory! Glory hallelujah!
         Glory! Glory hallelujah! His truth is marching on!

        I have seen him in the watch fires of a hundred circling camps;
        They have builded him an alter in the evening dews and damps;
        I have read his righteous sentence in the dim and flaring lamps;
        His day is marching on.

Chorus

        I have read a fiery gospel, writ in burnished rows of steel;
        "As ye deal with my contemners, so with you my grace shall deal";
        Let the hero, born of woman, crush the serpent with his heel;
        Since God is marching on.

Chorus

        In the beauty of the lilies Christ was born across the sea.
        With a glory in his bosom that transfigures you and me;
        As he died to make men holy, let us die to make men free;
        While God is marching on.

Chorus

DIXIE

Daniel Decatur Emmett composed "Dixie" (he called it "Dixie's Land") as a "walk around" to be performed by a minstrel show company in 1859. It became instantly popular and it's charm and vitality are undiminished these many years later. It was Abraham Lincoln's favorite song. Jefferson Davis had it played at his Inauguration and the southern troops naturally chose it for it's line "I'll take my stand to live and die in Dixie". The origin of the word "Dixie" for the southland is unknown as is the birth of the word "Yankee".

The Confederacy's anthem was written by a Yankee and an abolitionist. Of his creation, Dan Emmett later said, "If I'd known to what use they were going to put my song, I'll be damned if I would have written it."

       I wish I was in the land of cotton.
       Old times there are not forgotten,
       Look away, look away, look away, Dixieland.
       In Dixieland where I was born in,
       Early on one frosty morning
       Look away, look away, look away, Dixieland!

Chorus Then I wish I was in Dixie Hooray! Hooray!
       In Dixieland I'll take my stand
       To live and die in Dixie.
       Away, away, away down south in Dixie.
       Away, away, away down south in Dixie.

       Old missus married Will the weaver
       William was a gay deciever,
       Look away! Look away! Look away, Dixieland
       But when he put his arms around her,
       He smiled as fierce as a forty pounder,
       Look away! Look away! Look away, Dixieland!

Chorus

       His face was sharp as a butcher's cleaver,
       But that did not seem to grieve her,
       Look away, Look away, Look away, Dixieland
       Old missus acted the foolish part,
       And died for a man that broke her heart,
       Look away, Look away, Look away, Dixieland!

Chorus

       Now here's a health to the next old missus,
       And all the gals that want to kiss us,
       Look away, Look away, Look away, Dixieland
       But if you want to drive away sorrow,
       Come and hear this song tomorrow
       Look away, Look away, Look away, Dixieland!

Chorus

       There's buckwheat cakes and injun batter,
       Makes you fat or a little fatter,
       Look away, Look away, Look away, Dixieland!
       Then hoe it down and scratch your gravel,
       To Dixieland I'm bound to travel,
       Look away, Look away, Look away, Dixieland!

Chorus

THE BATTLE CRY OF FREEDOM

Early in the war, inspired by Lincoln's call for troops, George F. Root wrote the words and music to "The Battle Cry of Freedom". The song in turn inspired the troops. Once during the Battle of the Wilderness when the northern line was buckling, the men of the Forty-Fifth Pennsylvania began to sing it through the crackle of gunfire. Their raised voices caused the Union Ninth Corps to stand firm. Root also wrote "Tramp, Tramp, Tramp, the Boys Are Marching" and "Just Before the Battle, Mother."

Yes, we'll rally round the flag, boys, we'll rally once again,
    Shouting the battle cry of freedom!
We will rally from the hillside, we'll gather from the plain,
    Shouting the battle cry of freedom!

Chorus   The Union, forever, hurrah! Boys, hurrah!
            Down with the traitor, up with the star;
            While we rally round the flag, boys, rally once again,
            Shouting the battle cry of freedom.

We will welcome to our numbers the loyal, true and brave,
    Shouting the battle cry of freedom;
And although they may be poor, not a man shall be a slave,
    Shouting the battle cry of freedom.

Chorus

We are springing to the call of our brothers gone before,
    Shouting the battle cry of freedom;
And we'll fill the vacant ranks with a million freemen more,
    Shouting the battle cry of freedom.

Chorus

So we're springing to the call from the east and from the west,
    Shouting the battle cry of freedom,
And we'll hurl the rebel crew from the land we love the best,
    Shouting the battle cry of freedom.

Chorus

THE BONNIE BLUE FLAG

Just as "The Battle Cry of Freedom" inspired the Union troops, so "The Bonnie Blue Flag" did the southern soldiers. Before the Confederate flag, the stars and bars, was adopted, the standard for rebel legions was the flag of South Carolina, the first state to secede, a blue flag with one star. No one knows who wrote the words and music. They are said to have originated in a New Orleans music hall based on "The Irish Jaunting Car".

We are a band of brothers, and native to the soil,
Fighting for our liberty, with treasure, blood and toil.
And when our rights were threatened, the cry rose near and far,
"Hurrah! For the Bonnie Blue Flag that bears a single star."

Chorus Hurrah! Hurrah! For southern rights hurrah!
         Hurrah! For the Bonnie Blue Flag that bears a single star.

As long as the old Union was faithful to her trust,
Like friends and like brothers, kind were we, and just;
But now, when Northern treach'ry attempts our rights to mar,
We hoist on high the Bonnie Blue Flag that bears a single star.

Chorus

First, gallant South Carolina nobly made her stand;
Then came Alabama, who took her by the hand;
Next, quickly Mississippi, Georgia and Florida
All raised on high the Bonnie Blue Flag that bears a single star.

Chorus

Ye men of valor, gather round the banner of the right,
Texas and fair Louisiana, join us in the fight;
Davis, our loved President, and Stephens, statemen rare,
Now rally round the Bonnie Blue Flag that bears a single star.

Chorus

And here's to brave Virginia, the Old Dominion State
With the young Confederacy at length has linked her fate;
Impelled by her example, now other states prepare
To hoist on high the Bonnie Blue Flag that bears a single star.

Chorus

Then cheer, boys, cheer and raise the joyous shout,
For Arkansas and North Carolina now have both gone out;
And let another rousing cheer for Tennessee be given
The single star of Bonnie Blue Flag has grown to be eleven.

LORENA

H.D. Webster wrote the music and J.P. Webster (no relation), who also wrote "Sweet By And By", wrote the words for the southern soldiers' favorite sweetheart song.

The years creep slowly by, Lorena,
The snow is on the grass again.
The sun's low down the sky, Lorena,
The frost gleams where the flow'rs have been.
But the heart throbs as warmly now,
As when the summer days were nigh,
Oh, the sun can never dip so low
A-down affection's cloudless sky.

A hundred months have passed, Lorena,
Since last I held that hand in mine,
And felt the pulse beat fast, Lorena,
Though mine beat faster far than thine.
A hundred months, 'twas flowery May,
When up the hilly slope we climbed,
To watch the dying of the day,
And hear the distant church bells chime.

We loved each other then, Lorena,
More than we ever dared to tell;
And what we might have been, Lorena,
Had but our lovings prospered well -
But then, 'tis past, the years are gone,
I'll not call up their shadowy forms;
I'll say to them, "Lost years, sleep on!
Sleep on, nor heed life's pelting storms."

The story of that past, Lorena
Alas, I care not to repeat,
The hopes that could not last, Lorena,
They lived, but only lived to cheat.

I would not cause e'en one regret
To rankle in your bosom now;
For "If we try, we may forget,"
Were words of thine long years ago.

Yes, these were words of thine, Lorena.
They burn within my memory yet;
They touched some tender chords, Lorena,
Which thrill and tremble with regret.
'Twas not thy woman's heart that spoke;
Thy heart was always true to me;
A duty, stern and pressing, broke
The tie which linked my soul with thee.

It matters little now, Lorena,
The past is in the eternal past;
Our heads will soon lie low, Lorena,
Life's tide is ebbing out so fast.
There is a future! O, thank God!
Of life this is so small a part!
'Tis dust to dust beneath the sod;
But there, up there, 'tis heart to heart.

****

AURA LEE

Homesick Union soldiers sang around their campfires of Lorena's northern counterpart, Aura Lee. Her words and music were written in 1861 by George R. Poulton and W.W. Fosdick.

As the blackbird in the spring, 'neath the willow tree,
Sat and piped, I heard him sing, sing of Aura Lee.
Aura Lee! Aura Lee! Maid of golden hair!
Sunshine came along with thee, swallows in the air.

On her cheek the rose was born, 'twas music when she spake;
In her eyes the rays of morn with sudden splendor break.
Aura Lee, Aura Lee, maid of golden hair,
Sunshine came along with thee, and swallows in the air.

Aura Lee, the bird may flee, the willow's golden hair
Swing through winter fitfully on cold and stormy air.
Yet if thine eyes I see, gloom will soon depart;
For to me, sweet Aura Lee is sunshine through my heart.

When the mistletoe was green amidst the winter's snows,
Sunshine in thy face was seen and kissing lips of rose.
Aura Lee, Aura Lee, take my golden ring;
Love and light return with thee and swallows with the spring.

GOOBER PEAS

Near the end of the war the southern troop supplies had dwindled almost to a vanishing point, but Johnny Reb still had a sense of humor. Besides nourishment, soldiers found amusement in the daily ration of peanuts.

        Sitting by the roadside on a summer's day,
        Chatting with my messmates, passing time away,
        Lying in the shadow, underneath the trees,
        Goodness, how delicious, eating goober peas.

Chorus Peas, peas, peas, peas, eating goober peas.
        Goodness, how delicious, eating goober peas.

        When a horseman passes, the soldiers have a rule:
        To cry out at their loudest: "Mister, here's your mule."
        But another pleasure, enchantinger than these,
        Is wearing out your grinders, eating goober peas.

Chorus

        Just before the battle, the general hears a row;
        He says: "The Yanks are coming, I hear their rifles now."
        He turns around in wonder, and what do you think he sees?
        The Tennessee Militia eating goober peas.

Chorus

        I think my song has lasted almost long enough,
        The subject's interesting, but the rhymes are mighty rough;
        I wish this war was over, when free from rags and fleas,
        We'd kiss our wives and sweethearts, and gobble goober peas.

MARCHING THROUGH GEORGIA

In 1865 Henry C. Work, an abolitionist song-writer, composed this song to commemorate Sherman's March. It was probably the most often heard song at the post-war camps of the Grand Army of the Republic.

Bring the good old bugle, boys, we'll sing another song,
Sing it with a spirit that will start the world along,
Sing it as we used to sing it fifty thousand strong.

Chorus   While we were marching through Georgia.
       Hurrah.   Hurrah.
           Hurrah.   Hurrah. We bring the jubilee!
       Hurrah.   Hurrah.
           Hurrah.   Hurrah. The flag that makes you free.
  So we sang the chorus from Atlanta to the sea,
  While we were marching through Georgia.

How the darkies shouted when they heard the joyful sound;
How the turkeys gobbled which our commissary found;
How the sweet potatoes even started from the ground.

Chorus

Yes, and there were Union men who wept with joyful tears,
When they saw the honored flag they had not seen for years;
Hardly could they be refrain'd from breaking forth in cheers.

Chorus

"Sherman's dashing Yankee boys will never reach the coast."
So the saucy rebels said, and 'twas a handsome boast;
Had they not forgot, alas, to reckon with the host.

Chorus

So we made a thorough fare for freedom and her train,
Sixty miles in latitude, three hundred to the main;
Treason fled before us, for resistance was in vain.

Chorus

WHEN JOHNNY COMES MARCHING HOME

Patrick Gilmore, an Irish-American bandmaster stationed in occupied New Orleans in 1863, composed "When Johnny Comes Marching Home" and it became an instant hit. Today we cherish it as a legacy of the Civil War.

When Johnny comes marching home again, Hurrah! Hurrah!
We'll give him a hearty welcome then, Hurrah! Hurrah!
The men will cheer, the boys will shout,
The ladies they will all turn out;

Chorus And we'll all feel gay when Johnny comes marching home,
And we'll all feel gay when Johnny comes marching home.

The old church bells will peal with joy. Hurrah! Hurrah!
To welcome home our darling boy, Hurrah! Hurrah!
The village lads and lasses say
With roses they will strew the way;

Chorus

Get ready for the jubilee. Hurrah! Hurrah!
We'll give the hero three times three. Hurrah! Hurrah!
The laurel wreath is ready now,
To place up on his royal brow;

Chorus

Let love and friendship on that day, Hurrah! Hurrah!
Their choicest treasures then display. Hurrah! Hurrah!
And let each one perform his part,
To feel with joy the warrior's heart;

Chorus

With malice toward none; with charity for all; with firmness in the right. As God gives us to see the right, let us strive on to finish the work we are in; to bind up the nation's wounds; to care for him who shall have borne the battle, and for his widow, and his orphan — to do all which may achieve and cherish a just, and lasting peace, among ourselves, and with all nations.

— Abraham Lincoln
Second Inaugural Address
March 4, 1865

****

Seven miles west of Durham, North Carolina, General Joseph E. Johnston met General William T. Sherman and surrendered the Army of Tennessee at the home of James Bennett (research indicates "Bennitt" is the original spelling). The two generals met three times at the Bennett farm before signing surrender terms on April 26, 1865, seventeen days after General Robert E. Lee's surrender at Appomattox. Johnston's surrender effectively ended hostilities in the Carolinas, Georgia and Florida. This proved to be the largest troop surrender of the American Civil War.

Theodore Davis, an artist with Harper's Weekly, sketched the generals and their escorts assembling at the Bennett farm, a neutral site located along a major road connecting Hillsborough with Durham.

INTERIOR OF **JAMES BENNETT'S** HOUSE—SCENE OF JOHNSTON'S SURRENDER, April 26, 1865.
Sketched by Davis.

Exterior and Interior views of James Bennett's farmhouse - sketches by artist Theodore R. Davis Harper's Weekly IX (May 27, 1865) p. 332

QUICK REFERENCE GUIDE TO CAMPAIGNS AND BATTLES OF THE CIVIL WAR

Allatoona, Georgia - October 5, 1864

Antietam - A decisive battle fought at Antietam Creek near Sharpsburg, Maryland. On September 7, 1862, General George McClellan checked an attempted invasion of the North by Lee's forces.

Appomattox Campaign, Virginia - March 29 - April 9, 1865

Appomattox Courthouse, Virginia - April 9, 1865 - General Robert E. Lee surrendered his Army of Northern Virginia to General Ulysses S. Grant and thus ended the Civil War.

Atlanta, Georgia, July 22, 1864 - Evacuated by the Confederates on September 1, 1864.

Atlanta Campaign, Georgia - May - September, 1864

Athens, Alabama - January 26, 1864 - September 24, 1864

Averysboro, North Carolina - March 16, 1865

Ball's Bluff (Leesburg), Virginia - October 21-22, 1861

Baton Rouge, Louisiana - July 27 - August 6, 1862

Bean's Station, Tennessee - December 14, 1863

Belmont, Missouri - November 7, 1861

Bentonville, North Carolina - March 19-21, 1865

Big Bethel (Bethel Church, Great Bethel), Virginia - June 10, 1861

Boonesboro, Missouri - November 7, 1862

Boonesboro, South Mountain, Maryland - September 14, 1862

Brandy Station, Fleetwood, Virginia - June 9, 1863

Bristoe, Virginia - October 14, 1863

Brownsville, Texas (Palmito Ranch) - May 12, 1865 - The last Battle of the war and ironically a Confederate victory.

Bull Run (See Manassas)

Cape Hatteras (See Fort Hatteras)

Carolinas Campaign - January 1 - April 26, 1865

Carthage, Missouri - July 5, 1861

Cedar Creek (Bell Grove), Virginia -October 19, 1864

Cedar Mountain (Slaughterhouse Mountain, Southwest Mountain), Virginia - August 9, 1864

Centerville, Virginia - July 21, 1861

Champion's Hill, Mississippi - May 16, 1863

Chancellorsville, Virginia - An important battle fought on May 2-3, 1863, at rural crossroads of Chancellorsville in which General Lee and his forces defeated General Hooker's army which outnumbered them more than two to one. The Confederate victory frustrated Union plans to occupy Richmond and made possible Lee's advance into the North. The price of victory was high, however, for one of the South's most brilliant and indispensable generals was mortally wounded at Chancellorsville. Stonewall Jackson, reconnoitering behind the enemy lines in the dark, was shot by his own troops in the confusing thickets of the wilderness.

Charleston, South Carolina, bombardment of August 21, 1863 and December 31, 1863; Charleston withstood the most violent repeated assaults throughout the war but the flag of the Confederacy waved over the port city until almost the end, February 18, 1865

Chattanooga, Tennessee - The Union army of the Cumberland was bottled up in Chattanooga after it's rout from the Battle of Chickamauga (Q.V.). The Confederates under General Braxton Bragg entrenched on Lookout mountain and in lines up Missionary Ridge, both south of the city. Generals Hooker, Sherman and "The Rock of Chickamauga" Thomas, under Grant's overall command, succeeded in taking Lookout Mountain on November 24-25, 1863, in what the war correspondents dubbed "The Battle Above the Clouds." The decisive move came when Union soldiers, under Sherman's orders to take the first-held trench on Missionary Ridge and hold, took that trench and swept over the top of the ridge in a wild mass surge of pent up energy and rage that drove the Southerners back into Georgia. The South lost the west that day and left way open to Atlanta.

Chickamauga - A creek in north Georgia with a Cherokee name meaning "River of Death" ran red with blood on September 19, 1863 in the battle with the highest percentage of casualties of the war. General Bragg caught General William Rosecran's army of Cumberland in a trap at Chickamauga and before the day was over the Union soldiers were streaming back to Chattanooga in a disorderly rout, Rosecran in their number. General George Thomas patched up a line and held through most of the day, earning himself the title, the Rock of Chickamauga. He too was at last forced to withdraw. The South won the day, but Bragg refused to follow up and destroy the Union army, he lost his chance to do so. Lincoln removed Rosecrans and brought in Grant from Mississippi to take over the mess in Tennessee. Grant revenged Chickamauga two months later at the Battle of Chattanooga. (Q.V.)

Cold Harbor, First, Virginia - (Gaine's Mill, Chickahominy) June 27, 1862

Cold Harbor, Second, Virginia - June 3, 1864

Columbia, Tennessee - November 24-27, 1864

Corinth, Mississippi - October 3-4, 1862

The Crater, Virginia - July 30, 1864

Cross Keys, Virginia - June 8, 1862

Cumberland Gap, Tennessee - Evacuated by Federals, September 17, 1862

Dalton, Georgia - May 9-13, 1864; surrendered, October 13, 1864
Dinwiddie Courthouse, Virginia - March 31, 1865
Fayetteville, North Carolina - April 22, 1861 and March 11-12, 1865
Fisher's Hill, Virginia - September 22, 1864
Five Forks, Virginia - April 1, 1865
Fort Donelson, Tennessee - February 12-16, 1862
Fort Fisher, North Carolina - December 24-25, 1864 and January 13-15, 1865
Fort Hatteras, North Carolina - August 18-19, 1861
Fort Henry, Tennessee - January 17-22, 1862
Fort Hindman, Arkansas - (Arkansas Post), January 4-17, 1863
Fort Jackson, Louisiana - April 18-28, 1862
Fort Monroe, Virginia - The site of much activity during the Civil War; (the Merrimac and the Monitor fought here) the Federals launched balloon operations, Lincoln visited often. The Confederate commissioners met here and finally on May 22, 1865 Jefferson Davis was imprisoned here.
Fredericksburg, Virginia - Fought on December 13, 1862 between Southern forces commanded by Lee and led by Longstreet and Jackson, and a Union army of three grand divisions under General Ambrose Burnside, whose objectives were to cross the Rappahannock. Take the high ground at Marye's Heights beyond the town and sweep on to Richmond. Lee anticipated his every move and repulsed his assaults. Union losses were staggering and they retreated, causing great depression in the North.
Front Royal, Virginia - May 23, 30, 31, 1862
Galveston, Texas - January 1, 1863, Union blockade fleet attacked.
Gettysburg, Pennsylvania - The "Turning Point" battle of the war, fought July 1-3, 1863 at Gettysburg between Lee's forces and the Union army commanded by General George Meade. Lee hoped by his invasion of the North to inflict a deep wound on the vulnerable Federals and dissuade them from another offensive in Virginia. He also hoped they might decide to recognize the independence of the Confederacy. He was not able to achieve any of these goals. Meade was not vulnerable; he chose the site for the battle and Lee was forced to stand and fight at Gettysburg, against the advice of Longstreet, he ordered a frontal attack on Meade's center line which became the gallant, tragic Pickett's charge. Symbolic of the "Lost Cause." Lee took all the blame for the carnage and ordered a retreat back to Virginia. Meade's army was too spent to pursue them. After the war's greatest battle, the Confederacy was doomed by it's manufacturing and transportation inadequacies.
Goldsboro, North Carolina - March 19, 1865
Grand Gulf, Mississippi - March 31, 1863
Groveton, Virginia - (Manassas Plains) August 29, 1862
Hampton Roads, Virginia - March 8-9, 1862/the famous Naval contest between the Ironclads, the Monitor and the Merrimac

Harper's Ferry, West Virginia - September 12-15, 1862
Helena, Arkansas - January 1, 1863/July 4, 1863
Holly Springs, Mississippi - July 1, 1862/November 13 & 28, 1862 and December 20, 1862
Island No. 10. Tennessee - April 7-8, 1862
Iuka, Mississippi - September 19, 1862
Jackson, Mississippi - July 10, 1863
Jackson, Tennessee - June 7, 1862
Jenkins' Ferry, Arkansas - April 30, 1864
Jonesboro, Georgia - August 31 - September 1, 1864
Kennesaw Mountain, Georgia - June 10, 1864 & July 3, 1864
Kentucky Campaign - August-October, 1862
Kernstown, Virginia - March 23, 1862 & July 24, 1864
Knoxville Campaign, Tennessee - November 17 - December 4, 1863
Leesburg - See Ball's Bluff
Lexington, Missouri - September 20, 1861
Little Rock, Arkansas - September 10, 1863
Lynchburg, Virginia - July 17-18, 1864
Malvern Hill, Virginia - July 1, 1862
Manassas, First - The first major encounter, also known as Bull Run, of the war, fought in Virginia on July 21, 1861 between Union forces under General McDowell and Confederates under Generals Beauregard and Johnston. After a hard five hour battle, the Southerners were in retreat, but one brigade stoodfast behind their leader General Thomas J. Jackson until reinforcements arrived and drove the Union from the field. This stand earned Jackson the nickname "Stonewall" by which he was known ever after. The Union retreat back to Washington caused dismay in the North and changed the "rebellion" into a Civil War.
Manassas, Second - Fought on the right bank of Bull Run on August 29 & 30, 1862 between Lee's forces and Union soldiers under General John Pope. The first day fighting was inconclusive, but on the second day the Federals were again driven back to Washington. Pope was sacked and Lee's path cleared for a march into Maryland to Antietam (Q.V.).
Manassas Junction, Virginia - January 7, 1862
Martinsburg, West Virginia - September 18, 1864
Maryland Campaign - September 9-10, 1862
Mechanicsville (Beaver Dam Creek) - The first battle in Lee's week long offensive known as the "Seven Days", fought on June 26, 1862 at Mechanicsville, Virginia. Though this first day was a failure (Stonewall Jackson did not arrive in time to help A.P. Hill's assault on Union General Fitz-John Porter's troops and Hill was severely repulsed), the "Seven Days" were a success for the Confederacy despite heavy losses. Lee drove McClellan back down the James River to Harrison's Landing, ending his Peninsular Campaign, and saved Richmond, once again. Not for another year would the Federals get as close again to the Confederate Capital.

Mill Springs (Fishing Creek), Kentucky - January 19, 1862

Milliken's Bend, Louisiana - June 7, 1863

Mine Run, Virginia - November 26-December 2, 1863

Mobile, Alabama - February 16-March 27, 1864 & May 4, 1865/Evacuated by Confederates on April 11, 1865

Mobile Bay, Alabama - August 5, 1864, Admiral Farragut's Union Fleet moved past the forts at the entrance and "Damn the torpedoes. Full speed ahead!" was the cry that sent them on past the string of mines. Farragut defeated the Confederates whose chief defender of the harbor was the Ironclad, Tennessee, under the command of Admiral Frank Buchanan, former head of Annanpolis. This victory opened the way for land attacks against the city which the Southerners held until after the surrender at Appomattox.

Monocacy, Maryland - July 9, 1864

Morgan's Raids, Kentucky - July 4-28, 1862/December 22-January 2, 1863/May 31-June 20, 1864

Morgan's Raids, Indiana - July 9-13, 1863

Morgan's Raids, Ohio - July 13-16, 1863

Murfreesboro, Tennessee - A bloody battle fought on several different days between December 31, 1862 and January 3, 1863 along the Stones River at Murfreesboro. The Southerners led by General Braxton Bragg seemed to win at first but finally withdrew after losing 38,000 men. The Federals were commanded by General Rosecrans who did not pursue the retreating Confederate Army.

Nashville, Tennessee - December 15-16, 1864

New Bern, North Carolina - March 14, 1862

New Madrid, Missouri - March 3-14, 1862

New Market, Virginia - June 13, 1862

New Orleans, Louisiana - April 25, 1862, Admiral Farragut and his navy ran past heavy artillery fire from Forts Jackson and St. Philip which guarded the mouth of the Mississippi. After a bloody encounter with the Confederate side wheel ram, Governor Moore, Farragut took New Orleans, a grave loss for the Confederacy.

Okalona, Mississippi - February 22, 1864

Olustee, Florida - February 20, 1864

Overland Campaign, Virginia - Summer, 1864

Paducah, Kentucky - March 25, 1864

Plantersville, Alabama - April 1, 1865

Pea Ridge (Elkhorn), Arkansas - March 6-8, 1862

Peachtree Creek, Georgia - July 20, 1864

Peninsular Campaign, Virginia - April-July, 1862

Pensacola, Florida - Evacuated by Confederates, May 9-12, 1862
Evacuated by Federals, March 20-24, 1863

Perryville, Kentucky - October 7-8, 1862

Petersburg, Virginia - June 15-18, 1864/Siege of June 15, 1864 - April 2, 1865

Palmito Ranch, Texas - See Brownsville

Pleasant Hill, Louisiana - April 9, 1864
Plymouth, North Carolina - April 17-20, 1864
Port Gibson, Mississippi - May 1, 1863
Port Hudson, Louisiana - May 21-July 8, 1863
Port Republic, Virginia - June 8-9, 1862
Port Royal, South Carolina - January 1, 1862/June 6, 1862-July 4, 1862
Prairie Grove, Arkansas - December 7, 1862
Rappahannock Station, Virginia - October 22, 1865
Resaca, Georgia - May 14-15, 1864
Rich Mountain, West Virginia - June 19, 1864/April 3 1865
Richmond, Kentucky - August 30, 1862
Richmond, Virginia - Siege of, June 19, 1864/April 3, 1865
Romney, West Virginia - January 10, 1862
Sabine Cross Roads (Mansfield), Louisiana - April 8-9, 1864
Savage's Station - June 29, 1862
Savannah Campaign, Georgia - November 15 - December 21, 1864
Savage's Station, Virginia - June 29, 1862
Sayler's Creek, Virginia - April 6, 1865
Selma, Alabama - April 2, 1865
Seven Days, Virginia - June 26-July 2, 1862 (Mechanicsville (Q.V.), Beaver Dam Creek, Gaines' Mill, First Cold Harbor, The Chickahominy, Savage's Station, Peach Orchard, Frayser's Farm, White Oak Swamp, Malvern Hill.)
Seven Pines (Fair Oaks), Virginia - May 31-June 1, 1862. General Joseph Johnston was wounded at this battle and removed from action. President Jefferson Davis named General Lee to replace him and Lee began to plan the counter-offense which became the Seven Days Battles.
Sharpsburg, Maryland - September 17, 1862 (See Antietam)
Shenandoah Valley Campaign, Virginia - June-November 1864 (Early's)
Shenandoah Valley Campaign, Virginia - April-June 1862 (Jackson's)
Shiloh, Tennessee - One of the bloodiest, most desperate and most controversial battles of the war, fought on April 6-7, 1862 at Shiloh Church near Pittsburg Landing on the Tennessee River. The Confederates led the attack under Generals Albert Sidney Johnston and Pierre Beauregard against General Ulysses S. Grant's army. Johnston bled to death from a wound while his own surgeon treated Union casualties. The first day the Confederates under Beauregard drove the Union back about a mile. Reinforcements arrived, however, and the Union was able to drive the Southerners into retreat to Corinth, Mississippi on the second day. Losses on each side reached over 10,000. During the two days the fighting also raged at Savannah and Crump's Landing on the Tennessee River.
South Mountain, Maryland - September 14, 1862

Spotsylvania Courthouse, Virginia - One of the bloodiest contests of the war, fought May 10-21, 1864, during the Wilderness Campaign in Virginia. General Grant attacked Lee's men in their entrenchments and was repulsed with great losses. Grant vowed to continue the assault if it took all summer and repeated this thrust at the "Bloody Angle". Lee drew back to an inner line and Grant, unable to pry him loose, went around his flank toward Richmond.

Springfield (Wilson's Creek), Missouri - August 10, 1861 and October 25, 1861

South Mountain - See Boonesboro

Stones River - See Murfreesboro

Tennessee Campaign - November-December 1864 (Hood's)

Tupelo, Mississippi - May 5, 1863/July 14-15, 1864

Tuscumbia, Alabama - April 16, 1862/February 22, 1863/April 24, 1863-April 26, 1863

Vicksburg, Mississippi - Bombarded: June 28, 1862/Campaign against - December 20, 1862 - January 3, 1863
This Mississippi city, perched high on bluffs above the Mississippi River was a major obstacle to Union control of the "Father of the Waters" after the taking of Ft. Donelson and New Orleans. After repeated unsuccessful attempts to take the city by water, Grant masterfully maneuvered his men down the western shore of the river and ferried them across below the city, then he marched up from below, east of the city where he came between Confederate armies in Vicksburg and those of General Johnston sent to Jackson to aid the city. He drove Johnston from the field at Champion's Hill, backed Pemberton into his fortified hold, the death trap of Vicksburg. Pemberton would not say "Die" and so Grant laid siege to the fortress city which finally fell at just the moment the South was losing Gettysburg, July 4, 1863. The Mississippi River was lost, the Confederacy split in two, never to be rejoined, and Lincoln at last had his checkmate for General Lee - Ulysses S. Grant. Three fatal blows, coming with Gettysburg, from which the South could not recover.

The Wilderness - A wild woodland near Fredericksburg, Virginia, the scene of much bloodshed. The Battle of the Wilderness was fought May 5-7, 1864 between the armies of Lee and Grant. In a confusing, disjointed and bloody confrontation, the Confederates repulsed a Union assault and counterattacked on the 6th. Grant pushed around Lee and headed for Spotsylvania Courthouse (Q.V.) a move which Lee anticipated.

Wilderness Campaign, Virginia - May-June, 1864

Wilmington, North Carolina - February 22, 1865

Winchester, Virginia - March 22-23, 1862/July 24, 1864/September 19, 1864

Yellow Tavern, Virginia - May 11, 1864, in a sharp encounter between the cavalries of Generals Stuart and Sheridan. Stuart was mortally wounded.

Yorktown, Virginia - April 5-May 4, 1862

SUGGESTED READING
History, Biography, Diaries

The Civil War, A Narrative, 3 Vols.	Shelby Foote
Storm Over the Land, A Profile of the Civil War	Carl Sandburg
A Short History of the Civil War, Ordeal By Fire	Fletcher Pratt
A Naval History of the Civil War	Howard P. Nash, Jr.
The Civil War Day By Day, An Almanac 1861-1865	E.B. Long
Lee's Lieutenants, 3 Vols.	Douglas Southall Freeman
Fighting Confederates	Curt Anders
Spies of the Confederacy	John Bakeless
Brave Men and Great Captains	R. Ernest Dupuy and Trevor N. Dupuy
To Appomattox, Nine April Days, 1865	Burke Davis
The Oxford History of the American People	Samuel Eliot Morison
Mr. Lincoln's Army	Bruce Catton
A Stillness at Appomattox	Bruce Catton
This Hallowed Ground	Bruce Catton
The Coming Fury	Bruce Catton
The Terrible Swift Sword	Bruce Catton
Never Call Retreat	Bruce Catton
The American Heritage Pictorial History of the Civil War	Narrative by Bruce Catton
Heroines of Dixie	Katherine M. Jones
Mary Chestnut's Civil War	Edited by C. Vann Woodward
The Women and the Crisis, Women of the North During the Civil War.	Agatha Young
The Wartime Papers of R.E. Lee	R.E. Lee
I Rode With Stonewall	Henry Kyd Douglas
Jefferson Davis	Hudson Strode
Grant, A Biography	William S. McFeely
The Ordeal of the Union, 8 Vols.	Allan Nevins
The Union Sundered, The Union Restored, Vols. 5 & 6, Life History of the United States	T. Harry Williams
A People's History of the Civil War	Pae Smith
A Pictorial History of the Negro in America	Langston Hughes Milton Meltzer

— AUTHOR —

Bio

JUDITH M. CHENEY, born in Harrodsburg, Kentucky, had ancestors on both sides in the Civil War. One great-grandfather served in the 6th Kentucky Cavalry U.S.A. under Thomas ("The Rock") at Chickamauga and Missionary Ridge, and with Wilson at Selma. His brother, who joined the Confederate army, died of typhoid fever, before seeing action. Another great-grandfather, a noncombatant rebel surgeon, treated the wounded from both Southern and Northern armies at the Battle of Perryville. Another relative raised a company of volunteers in the Yazoo Delta north of Vicksburg. In Mrs. Cheney's childhood home, Civil War stories were family table-talk ("As if it had happened just before I was born".) "Yankees and Confederates" was an on-going neighborhood game. A graduate of Northwestern University, she attended the Sorbonne, University of Paris, has worked as an artist-writer on The Milwaukee Sentinel, The Chicago Daily News, and The Palm Beach Post. She lives with her husband and son in a log cabin in Horse Shoe, N.C., where she paints, gardens, raises goats and studies American history and literature.